NEW HORIZONS

science 5-16

KEY STAGE 2

What is it made of?

Jacqueline Dineen

CAMBRIDGE
UNIVERSITY PRESS

Published by the Press Syndicate of the
University of Cambridge
The Pitt Building, Trumpington Street,
Cambridge CB2 1RP
40 West 20th Street, New York,
NY 10011-4211, USA
10 Stamford Road, Oakleigh,
Melbourne 3166, Australia

© Cambridge University Press 1992

First published 1992

Designed by Steve Knowlden and Pardoe
Blacker Publishing Ltd, Shawlands Court,
Newchapel Road, Lingfield, Surrey RH7 6BL
Illustrated by Annabelle Brend, Dawn Brend,
Chris Forsey, Jenny Mumford and Paul Williams

Printed in Great Britain by Scotprint Ltd,
Musselburgh, Scotland.

A catalogue record for this book is
available from the British Library

ISBN 0 521 39756 1

Acknowledgements

The author and publishers would like to thank the following
for supplying additional information: British Alcan Aluminium
plc, British Steel plc, Brooke Bond Foods Ltd, DRG Plastics,
English Woodlands Timber, Redland Aggregates Ltd, Sappi
Graphics, Alison Stevenson Public Relations, Scandia Hus Ltd,
Southern Water plc, Steel Can Recycling Information Bureau,
Talc de Luzenac.

Photographic credits

t=top b=bottom c=centre l=left r=right
Cover: ZEFA

5 Shell Photographic Library; 6t, 6b, 7tl, 7tr, 7c, 7b
British Steel plc; 9t Wales Tourist Board; 9b Ed Bock/
ZEFA; 11c, 11b George Wimpey plc; 13t Wedgwood;
13b Portfolios/Dartington Crystal Limited; 14t, 14c,
14b, 15 Hepworth Building Products; 18t Trevor Hill;
18b Penrose Pictures; 19t Trevor Hill; 19b Penrose
Pictures; 20tl Design Museum; 20r, 21l ZEFA;
21r Addis/Munro & Forster Public Relations; 22t The
Hutchison Library; 23l, 23r The International Coffee
Organisation; 27t Trevor Hill; 27c ZEFA; 27b Trevor Hill;
29 Jon Williams; 30t Bryn Colton/Birds Eye Walls/Hall
Harrison Cowley Advertising; 30c Maureen Ashley/
The Anthony Blake Photo Library; 30b The Anthony
Blake Photo Library; 31t, 31c Trevor Hill; 31b, 32 ZEFA;
33 Wales Tourist Board; 34 Anthony Bannister/NHPA;
35 Nigel Cattlin/Holt Studios International; 36 Hilly
James/The Hutchison Library; 37tl, 37tr, 37c Images of
India; 37b E. Jefferies & Sons Ltd; 39tl, 39c ICI Fibres;
39tl Courtaulds plc; 41bl ZEFA; 41br Surrey Fire and
Rescue Service; 42t, 42c, 42b Ideal Standard Ltd;
44t, 44b Krov Menuhin/Seaphot Limited; 45t Jon
Williams; 45b Trevor Hill; 46t Images; 46b Talc de
Luzenac; 47 The Body Shop International plc; 52t Selo-
Bollans Ltd; 52b Mono Containers Ltd; 53 Trevor Hill;
54 Mark Boulton/ICCE; 57tl Andy Purcell/ICCE;
57tr Cleanaway Ltd; 57b Sally and Richard Greenhill;
58l, 58c, 58r, 59l, 59c, 59r James River Fine Papers
Group; 60t Jon Williams; 61b Steel Can Recycling
Information Bureau.

Contents

Introduction

Nearly everything around you is made from materials which come from the Earth. We call these 'raw' materials. Some have to be changed before we can use them. Plastic is made from oil found deep in the Earth.

Beneath the surface

Rocks are sandwiched between each other in layers. We can use these rocks for building and for making building materials.

Look at all the things around you. What are they made of?

Buried among the layers of rock are metals such as iron and copper. Can you find out how we use these? There are precious metals like gold and silver, and precious stones like diamonds. Materials such as rock and metals are **minerals**.

We need **fuel** for machinery. The fuels we use most — coal, oil and gas — also come from these rocks. Find out more about them in the *New Horizons* book, *Energy, forces and communication*.

Find out more about rocks in the *New Horizons* book, *Land, water and air*.

4

Finding the materials

Often, you cannot see where minerals, coal, oil and gas are buried. **Geologists** are people who study rocks and minerals in the Earth. They know which types are found near each other. They make a **survey** or close study of an area to find out about the minerals under the surface. When they find a useful mineral, it is brought to the surface by drilling or mining.

This geologist is studying a sample of rocks from beneath the Earth's surface in Indonesia.

Materials from plants

Trees provide wood for building, fuel and furniture. The paper for the pages of this book is made from wood.

Fibres for making cotton cloth come from a plant. Fibres are thin threads. They can be twisted together to make a longer, thicker thread which can be woven into cloth.

Some dyes and medicines are made from plants.

Some materials come from animals. Wool is one. Can you think of others?

We collect some materials from the Earth. We plant others specially. Farmers grow plants for food. We plant forests for wood. Even so, there are sometimes not enough materials to go round. This is because there are so many people in the world. Also, it can be difficult to get materials to them.

5

More about: building pp10-11 fabrics pp40-41 food pp22-31

Using materials

Some materials can be used as they are. Others have to be worked on or mixed together. Wood is a natural material which can be used as it is. A wooden table is **manufactured** from a natural material. It began as a tree. Stone is a building material. It can be used as it is. Bricks are also building materials. They are manufactured from clay which has to be shaped and then baked hard.

Plastic and nylon are **synthetic** manufactured materials. They are made by combining substances which come from oil.

New building materials

Minerals can be combined together to make new materials.

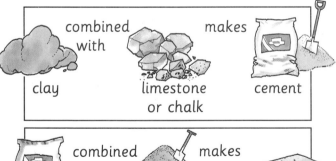

clay — combined with — limestone or chalk — makes — cement

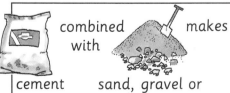

cement — combined with — sand, gravel or other crushed rocks — makes — concrete

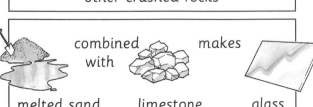

melted sand — combined with — limestone — makes — glass

Making steel

Steel is an important material in our modern world. It is used to make machinery which manufactures nearly every object we use. Steel is made from a mineral, iron **ore**.

1

The hot metal is poured into another furnace where it is made **pure**.

Iron ore is mixed with coke (made from coal) and limestone in the top of a **blast furnace**. A white-hot blast of air melts the iron. A pool of **molten** metal (called 'hot metal') collects at the bottom. The molten rock and coke float on top of it.

iron ore

limestone

At the casting machine, the liquid steel runs into a mould cooled with water.

It is then pulled downwards to form long bars or slabs.

Can you find out how steel is used in farming, transport, as packaging, in your home, in sport?

When these have cooled, they are ready to be made into products for sale.

The steel is poured into a ladle. A huge crane takes it to be **cast**.

Using up materials

Some of the materials we use have taken a long time to form. Coal and oil are the remains of animals and plants which died millions of years ago. Huge trees in the rain forests of South America, Africa and South East Asia have taken hundreds of years to grow. We are using up these materials very fast, and they cannot be replaced.

Today, people are looking at ways of saving materials. Paper, metal and glass are often thrown away and wasted. They can be recycled or re-used.

More about: clay pp12-13 glass p13 recycling pp57-61

Materials around us

The first humans did not have transport to carry materials and goods all over the world. They had to make do with the materials around them.

Early people moved around looking for food. At night, they needed shelter. Sometimes they slept in caves.

By leaning poles together, they made the frame for a shelter. Grass and leaves, or animal skins were used to cover the frame.

Sometimes, they built walls from loose rocks and made a roof of branches and leaves.

Later, they discovered how to make shelters from branches using leaves to keep out the rain. Simple tools were made to trim the branches.

As people settled in one place, they needed more permanent huts and houses. Sticky clay soils go hard when they dry. People shaped clay into bricks which they dried in the sun. Holes were left to let in the light. Holes also let in cold air, so in cool countries they were small. The rooms were dark.

People also learned to cut and shape stone for building. Today, you can see towns and villages where most of the buildings are built from the local stone, such as sandstone or flint.

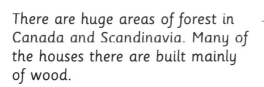

There are huge areas of forest in Canada and Scandinavia. Many of the houses there are built mainly of wood.

Houses around the world

In different parts of the world, people have used local materials to build their houses.

In parts of Africa it is very hot. Houses have thick mud walls. Mud bakes hard in the sun and the thick walls keep out the heat.

North American Indians made wigwams from buffalo skins stretched over poles.

Other tribes built shelters from adobe – bricks made from mud and straw and baked in the sun.

The Inuit (Eskimos) live in the Arctic. Some Inuit used to build igloos from blocks of snow. Others live in tents made from the skins of animals they have hunted.

Some people who live in the **tropical** rain forests build houses from the wood and leaves growing there.

Many people no longer live in these traditional houses. They use materials from other places.

9

More about: bricks pp10, 14-15 building pp10-11, 16-17

Choosing the best material

Today, we can choose which materials to use. Bricks or concrete can be made in one place and used somewhere else. Wood can be taken out of the forests and shipped around the world. People can decide which is the best material for the job they are doing.

What would happen to a wall if the joins between the bricks went up the wall in a straight line?

Houses are often built from bricks. Bricks are small and easy to handle. When they are **bonded** or stuck together in certain patterns, they make a strong wall. Blocks of stone are bonded in the same way.

Older, tall buildings like cathedrals have very thick walls. If today's skyscrapers were built like this, there would be no room inside!

Forces on the walls

Walls have to be strong. The force of strong winds could push them over. They have to support the whole weight of the building. (These are called the load-bearing walls.) The roof and floors press down hard. The bricks or blocks at the bottom could crumble if the weight is too great. If the walls are thicker at the bottom, there are more bricks or stones to support the weight.

Brick and stone flake and crumble as they get older, and water and air makes steel **rust**. Concrete does none of these – in fact, it gets stronger as it gets older.

Liquid concrete sets hard, so it can be cast into the best shapes for the job. Casting is like pouring jelly into a mould. Concrete is used for structures such as bridges which have to bear a lot of weight.

Modern office or apartment blocks are often made of concrete with a steel framework to support them.

Using aluminium

Aluminium is a light metal which does not rust like iron, or rot like wood. It is used for window frames, railings, lamp-posts and traffic signs. It is the best material for aeroplanes and boats built for speed. It is also used to make drinks cans and cooking foil!

Aluminium can be mixed with another metal such as copper to make it stronger.

More about: aluminium p60 bricks pp8-9, 14-15 concrete pp6, 17

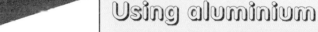

Materials from the

Stone

Then, a hole is bored into the stone and some explosives are put in. The explosion breaks the stone into pieces.

Stone is removed from the ground by **quarrying**. First, the top layer of earth and rock is removed.

Clay

Some types of excavator, called draglines, can dig deep down.

Clay is soft. It is dug out of pits by an **excavator**.

Sand and gravel

Sand and **gravel** are needed to make concrete. They are dug out of pits. When there is no sand or gravel left, some pits are filled with water and used for water sports, or as a nature reserve. Others are filled with soil for farming or building on.

ground

The stone pieces are taken to be shaped into building blocks or crushed to make cement.

The clay is loaded on to a conveyor belt or into trucks and taken to a brickworks or to a cement factory.

Baking clay

Early people made clay pots and put them into the camp fire to harden. About 7000 years ago, potters in the Middle East and Egypt began 'firing' their pots in ovens. These were the first **kilns**.

The Sumerians, who lived in the Middle East, wrote on tablets of soft clay. The tablets were then baked hard in the sun.

Loading pottery into a modern kiln.

Making glass

Sand contains tiny **crystals** called **silica**. If the sand is heated to a very high **temperature** and kept hot, the silica will melt. The melted silica forms **transparent** drops of glass. The drops **fuse** or stick together to form liquid glass which can be made into different shapes. Crushed limestone is added to make the glass hard and strong when it is cooled.

13

More about: clay pp6, 8, 14-15 glass pp6, 61 stone pp9, 10

Making bricks

First, clay is put into a machine where rollers grind it to crush any stones.

Today, most moulded bricks are made by machines which can shape several bricks at once. Bricks are also shaped by **extrusion**.

Next, the clay goes into a mixer where other ingredients are added to change the colour or make it stronger.

Shaping the bricks

For hundreds of years, bricks were shaped by hand-moulding. The moulders threw the clay into brick-shaped moulds, pushing it into each corner. They smoothed the top and turned the bricks out of the moulds. Hand-moulding is still used to make bricks in special shapes.

Clay is put in one end of the machine and forced out through a rectangular hole at the other end. It comes out as a long column of clay. Wires cut it into separate bricks.

The bricks are put on racks in a dryer. Air is blown round them. They would crack if the air was too hot at first. The air starts cool and moist and gets hotter and drier as the bricks harden.

Firing the bricks

The bricks are put into a kiln which fires them until they are hard. Brick-making kilns are huge. Thousands of bricks can be fired at a time.

A continuous kiln has several separate chambers. The first is filled with bricks which are fired by hot gases. While they are cooled and removed, the next chamber is loaded with bricks, and so on.

In a tunnel kiln, cars loaded with bricks pass through a tunnel. Here, they are fired and then cooled.

Different bricks

Most bricks have to be exactly the same size and shape so that they will fit together properly.

Sometimes, special shapes are needed. Different clays produce bricks of different colours. Bricks can be made to give the right strength or appearance. Engineering bricks are very strong. They are used to build railway tunnels and underground **sewers**.

Facing bricks are **finished** in special ways. They are used where the appearance is important.

15

More about: bricks pp10-11 building pp10-11, 16-17 clay pp12-13

Building a house

The roof is made of tiles laid on wooden rafters.

A carpenter fits the wooden parts such as floorboards and rafters.

A surveyor makes a detailed plan of the building plot.

Pipes for water and drains are laid under the house. A plumber connects up the taps and fits radiators for central heating.

A bricklayer builds the walls.

The bricks are joined together with mortar. This is a mixture of sand and cement.

inner wall

outer wall

cavity (space)

The ground is levelled with a bulldozer. The builder digs a wide trench and fills it with concrete to make the **foundations**.

If the soil is soft, the foundations have to go deeper to support the house. On very soft ground, houses are built on a raft of concrete which goes under the whole building.

aluminium or plastic-coated window frames

16 An architect draws a plan of the house.

Tiles are fired clay, or concrete. They overlap so water cannot get in through the gaps.

Warm air rises, so the loft is lined with insulating material to stop heat escaping through the roof.

Paint protects the walls and woodwork and makes them look attractive.

An electrician puts in wiring.

Metal ties, twisted so that water cannot run along them, strengthen the walls.

Some cavities are filled with plastic foam **insulation** to stop heat escaping.

Bricks are **porous**. A damp-proof course stops damp from the ground rising up into the walls. A thin layer of waterproof plastic is put between two layers of bricks.

Testing materials

Set up an experiment to see how much water bricks soak up. How did you do this? What did you find?

What materials could you use for insulation? Design a test to see which materials keep heat in best.

Cement and concrete

Cement is made by mixing clay with water and crushed limestone or chalk. The mixture is heated in a kiln. Solid lumps form which are ground into cement powder.

Cement powder is mixed to a paste with water. It soon begins to set hard, so it has to be used quickly. On its own, cement breaks easily.

Concrete is stronger. It is made by mixing **aggregates** (sand, gravel, flint, or crushed rocks) with cement powder and water. Concrete can be made even stronger by **reinforcing** it. Liquid concrete is poured into a cast with steel rods in it. The concrete sets round the rods.

Pre-stressed concrete is also strong. Steel wires are stretched through the concrete and kept very tight until it has set. When the wires are released, they **compress** or squash the concrete together which makes it stronger.

17

More about: cement p6 concrete pp6, 11, 13 water supply pp50-51

Using wood

Wood is the oldest building material. It is warm, attractive and **flexible**. It is suitable for floorboards, which have to bend under weight without breaking.

Problems with wood

Wood can rot if water gets into it and does not dry out. Wood also burns easily, so there is a risk of fire in wooden buildings. Woodworm and other small animals sometimes live in wood and eat it.

When wood fills with water, it **expands** or gets bigger and shrinks back when it dries out. This makes doors difficult to close when they are wet. Sometimes the wood becomes **warped** or twisted.

*Wood can be **treated** to protect it. It can be covered with substances which kill fungi and protect it from the weather.*

Types of wood

Hardwoods grow slowly, so they are expensive. They are strong and come from trees like teak, mahogany and oak.

oak elm beech

Preparing wood

When a tree is chopped down, it is cut into logs and taken to a **sawmill**. Here it is sawn into planks.

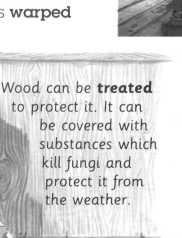

Softwoods come from pines and firs. They grow quickly and the wood is cheaper. Softwood is not as strong as hardwood and it takes in water more easily.

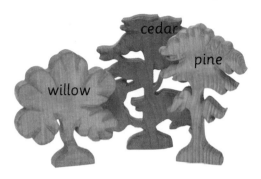

willow

cedar

pine

The wood has to be dried out or **seasoned** carefully so that it does not warp, crack or shrink. The planks are stacked in the open air or in kilns to dry. In a kiln, warm air is blown round the planks so they dry easily.

Building ships

The first 'boats' were probably logs of wood. People sat on them and paddled through the water with their hands. Then people tied logs together to make rafts or hollowed them out to make 'dug-out' canoes. People still make dug-out canoes in the rain forests of Africa and South America. Wood was the main ship-building material for thousands of years. Oak was used to build the galleons that first sailed round the world.

The lightest wood is balsa which grows in South America. In ancient Peru, people made light balsa-wood rafts and attached sails to them. In 1947, Thor Heyerdahl made a balsa-wood raft, the *Kon-Tiki*. He showed that the Peruvians could have sailed on rafts across the Pacific Ocean to the South Sea islands. Can you find out more about the *Kon-Tiki* expedition?

More about: building materials pp6, 8-15   window frames pp11, 16, 48

Plastic

Imagine a world without plastic! The first type was called celluloid. It was produced in 1862.

One of the first celluloid toys.

Today, plastic is used in many different ways. The word 'plastic' means something that can be moulded or shaped.

Clay can be moulded, but only keeps its shape if it is fired.

Pottery and china are made from clay. When they are fired, they become so hard that they break when you drop them.

Plasticene can be moulded, but it stays soft and changes its shape easily.

Using plastic

One type of plastic is hard and rigid (does not bend). First, the plastic is heated until it is soft. Then it is moulded and heated once more. This time, it hardens and keeps its shape. It cannot be softened again.

When oil comes out of the ground, it goes to a **refinery**. Here, it is separated into different parts to make oil products such as petrol and paraffin. The parts for making plastic are separated out at the same time.

The other type is more flexible (bendy). It is softened to shape it, but it is not reheated. As it cools, it hardens and keeps its shape, but it softens again if it gets too hot.

Light fittings and plugs are made from rigid plastic. Polythene is made from flexible plastic. Look around the kitchen for things made from plastic. How many of each type can you find? What about the washing-up bowl?

Products made from plastic are shaped by extrusion while the plastic is soft. Can you guess what is being made in the picture on the left?

21

More about: clay pp6, 8, 12-13 oil p5 oil products p39

What we eat

We need to eat to live. Early people had to find food from the animals and plants around them. They learned which plants tasted good and which were poisonous or tasted unpleasant. They killed animals and ate the meat raw. It was very tough to chew.

Foods around the world

Many countries have traditional dishes. These are usually made from ingredients which are grown or produced locally.

Long ago, people found that fire changed their food. It often tasted better and was easier to chew. They learned how to soften vegetables by cooking them in water. The people in the picture above are from Brazil. They still cook over open fires.

People all over the world can enjoy these dishes in restaurants and 'take-aways' which specialise in cooking from different countries.

Often people buy the ingredients to make these dishes at home.

Italy is well-known for its **pasta**, such as spaghetti with a meat sauce.

In Mexico, people use hot chilli peppers to spice their food.

In India, people eat spicy curries and rice.

Importing food

Today, we can **import** food from all over the world. We can buy the food fresh. We can freeze many foods to keep them fresh for months. There are factories where the food is **processed** or altered to preserve it or make it more convenient to use.

The fruits of the coffee plant each contain two beans. Machines remove the beans which are dried in the sun.

The dried beans are packed in sacks ready for **export**.

Japan is a fishing country. The Japanese eat more fish than anything else.

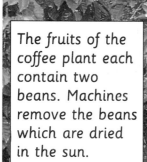

Chinese dishes often include rice, fish, meat, vegetables and noodles.

We need to eat a mixture of foods to stay healthy – a balanced **diet**. In some parts of the world, people grow food for their families because they cannot afford to buy it. They have to grow crops best suited to the land and **climate**.

The tropical grasslands of Africa are very dry. The main food crops are maize, yams and cassava, but these do not provide a good diet on their own.

More about: cooking pp24-29 fire p24 preserving food pp30-31

Changing food by cooking

Cooking improves some foods and makes them easier and more pleasant to eat. It can also destroy the goodness in food.

Meat, fish and vegetables such as potatoes can be fried or roasted in hot fat. Many people enjoy fried foods, but too many are bad for you. Fat hardens in your **arteries** and makes them clog up. Your blood cannot pass through easily. This puts a strain on your heart as it tries to pump blood round your body.

Find out more about healthy eating in the *New Horizons* book, *Look you! Look me!*

Making fire

Fires may happen when lightning strikes trees and bushes. Early people used burning twigs to light their own fires. They used flint tools. Striking flints together produces sparks, so they could start twigs burning themselves.

Boiling food for too long can destroy some vitamins.

Fish and vegetables can be steamed. The food cooks in the steam from boiling water, but it is not put into the water.

Cooking times are important. Roasting and grilling soften meat if the cooking time is right.

Grilling is a more healthy way to cook because it does not use extra fat.

Some fruit and vegetables can be baked. They are cooked in their skins. This keeps the vitamins in.

25

More about: fire p22 changing food pp26-31 cooking pp22-23, 26-29

Air in food

Air changes food by making it rise or swell.

1 When you bake a cake, you beat the fat, sugar and eggs together to trap air bubbles in the mixture.

2 The sugar crystals become coated with fat and stick together. This strengthens the mixture and helps to keep the air in.

4 If you are making biscuits or pastry, you use plain flour. The mixture stays flat when you bake it.

If you bake a cake with plain flour, you add a pinch of baking powder.

Baking powder contains bicarbonate of soda.

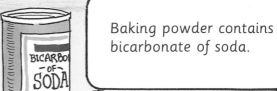

Did you know...?

Meringues are made from egg whites and sugar. Egg whites become white and stiff when air is beaten into them. Meringues are cooked in a cool oven. They do not rise but turn hard and crisp.

3 A cake is baked in a hot oven. The heat makes the air bubbles expand and the mixture rises.

5 When bicarbonate of soda is heated in the oven, it gives off **carbon dioxide** gas. This puts bubbles into the mixture.

6 Self-raising flour is plain flour with bicarbonate of soda added in the packet.

Mexican *tortillas* are made from **maize** flour. Indian *chapatis* and Greek *pitta* bread are made without yeast from wheat flour. Can you find these in the picture?

Fizzy drinks

Fizzy drinks are made by mixing fruit juices or other flavourings with fizzy water. The water is given its fizz by pumping carbon dioxide into it. Fizzy water is called 'carbonated' water.

Making bread

Most bread is made by adding **yeast** to the dough. Yeast is a type of **fungus**. Warm air makes the yeast fill the dough with bubbles of carbon dioxide gas. The dough is left in a warm place until it has swollen. Then it is shaped into loaves and left to rise again before baking. The heat of the oven kills the yeast and stops the bread swelling.

yeast

27

More about: baking pp24-25 eggs pp28, 31 water pp30, 50-51

More ways to change food

Heat does not have the same effect on all foods.

When water gets very cold, it freezes. It changes from a liquid to a solid block of ice. Many foods contain water. That is why they can be frozen.

Butter, chocolate and ice cream melt in heat. The heat of the sun is enough.

Some foods need a higher temperature before they change. They have to be cooked. Cheese melts and turns stringy.

Eggs go solid when they are cooked. When an egg fries, the yolk is runny and the white is transparent at first. As it cooks, the white turns solid and white and the yolk hardens. Liquids boil in the same way as water.

Cooking softens vegetables and fruit, and changes the flavour. Meat and fish become easier to chew.

Food and water

Foods change in different ways when they are mixed with water. Some need water *and* heat before they change.

Water itself changes when it is heated and cooled. If you boil water, it **evaporates**, or changes from a liquid to a gas.

Things which change in water

If you stir salt into water, the grains of salt seem to disappear. They **dissolve**. Some substances, such as coffee, dissolve well in hot water. Powdery foods like flour

Jelly cubes dissolve into a liquid when you add boiling water.

When the jelly cools, it changes back into a solid.

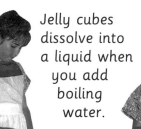

Making butter

Butter is made from milk. In some bottles of milk, there is a layer of cream at the top, made up of drops of fat. If you take the cream off . . .

. . . and shake it hard, the drops of fat form a solid mass. This is butter. The liquid that is left is called buttermilk.

Cream is put into a machine which shakes it. This is called 'churning', from the days when butter was made in **churns**.

Most butter has salt added. It no longer looks or tastes like milk. Shaking has changed the cream completely.

People who do not want to eat too much fat choose skimmed or semi-skimmed milk.

Skimmed milk has had all the cream removed. Semi-skimmed milk has had some of the cream removed.

can form a paste when they are mixed with water.

Sometimes water is used to draw out the flavour of a food. When you make a pot of tea, the flavour of the tea-leaves dissolves into the boiling water. Using water in this way is called 'infusion'.

Tests with water

Which substances dissolve in water? What about sugar? Do you think you could take the salt or sugar back out of the water?

Some things will not mix with water. Try mixing cold water with cold cooking oil. What happens?

29

More about: cooking pp24–27 evaporation p49 fat pp24–25

Preserving food

When people began to grow their own food, they found that they had plenty at some times of the year and not enough at others. They found ways of **preserving** food until they needed it. All change the food in some way.

Meat and fish could be 'salted' . . .

Bacteria need water and warmth to become active and multiply. They cannot grow if food is frozen. Freezing is a popular way of preserving because it does not alter the flavour much.

Chicken and some other foods need careful **defrosting** otherwise bacteria which cause food poisoning may not be killed when the food is cooked. Food should never be frozen again after defrosting because it can be bad for you.

. . . or hung in the smoke from a fire.

Sugar is a natural preservative. The sugar in jam preserves the fruit.

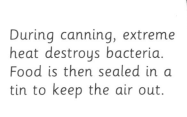

During canning, extreme heat destroys bacteria. Food is then sealed in a tin to keep the air out.

Pickling food

People found they could keep fruit and vegetables after the harvest by pickling them in vinegar.

Vinegar is an **acid**. It is made from beer, cider or wine which contain alcohol. Wine is usually made from grapes which contain sugar. Yeast is added to the crushed grapes. It works on the sugar and turns it into alcohol. This process is called **fermentation**.

Harmless bacteria are added to the liquid to turn it into sour vinegar.

Taking the water out

Bacteria are living things. You can see them only with a microscope, but they are all around us. Some make food go bad. They need water to develop.

Drying all the water out of food is one way of preserving it. You can buy dried fruit (prunes are dried plums, raisins are dried grapes), vegetables, meat, fish and herbs for flavouring food.

Some dried foods have to be soaked to put the water back in before they are cooked.

Changing food

Can you change a hard-boiled egg back to a raw egg? What happens to a slice of bread when you toast it? Does it become a different food? Can you change it back to plain bread again? Do jellies melt when they are warmed again?

Steam changes to water when it is cooled. What happens to melted butter and chocolate when they are cooled? Are they exactly as they were before?

31

More about: cans pp60-61 fresh food pp23, 24-25 yeast p27

What we wear

Clothes keep you warm in cold weather. They also protect your body from the sun in hot weather.

In tropical climates, it is often hot. People can wear the same type of clothes all the year round.

Where do fabrics come from?

Some fabrics come from plants and animals. These are natural fabrics. Cotton comes from the cotton plant. It is cool and comfortable to wear in hot weather. Wool comes from sheep. It is a warm material used for making sweaters and gloves.

We also make clothes from manufactured materials such as nylon and polyester. These are often cheaper, more hard-wearing and easier to wash and iron than natural materials.

In Britain and other **temperate** climates, the weather changes a lot. In winter it can be very cold, with snow and ice. In summer it can be hot. Clothes can be made from different materials or **fabrics**.

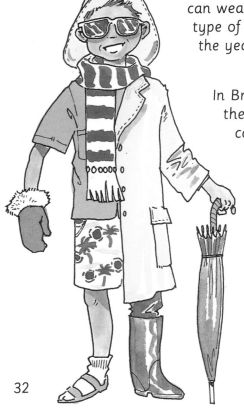

Silk, leather and rubber are natural materials. Can you find out where they come from?

The first clothes

The earliest people lived in Africa and did not need to wear clothes. As they moved into cooler parts of the world, they needed something to keep them warm.

People began to **domesticate** animals for meat and milk about 10 000 years ago. They found that they could twist long strands of sheep's wool together to make a thread.

They killed animals for food and had to skin them before they could eat the meat. They wore the warm furry skins from larger animals such as sheep, goats and deer.

About 9000 years ago, people in the Middle East began to **spin** wool using two sticks called a spindle and a distaff. A bundle of wool was held on the distaff. The strands were twisted together on the spindle.

People learned to weave the thread into cloth on a loom. A loom is a frame with threads running lengthways in it. The weaver passes another thread under and over them. You can try spinning and weaving for yourself!

33

More about: nylon p39 silk pp36–37 rubber pp35, 41

Materials from plants

Some plants produce fibres which can be spun into thread. Cotton comes from the fluffy seeds of the cotton plant. Linen is made from fibres in the stem of the flax plant. Hemp from Asia and jute from India can be made into rope and coarse cloth.

Making cotton

Cotton is a strong, smooth cloth worn by people all over the world. The cotton plant grows in a warm climate where there is plenty of sun.

The cotton plant is a flowering bush. When the flowers die, the cotton boll (a small seed pod) swells and bursts open. Inside is a mass of fluffy fibres which are made into cotton.

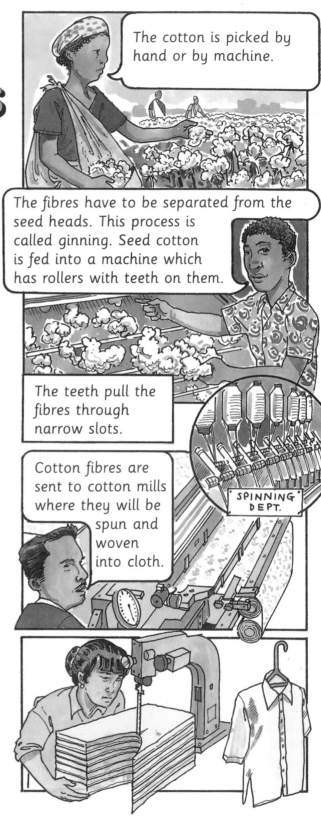

The cotton is picked by hand or by machine.

The fibres have to be separated from the seed heads. This process is called ginning. Seed cotton is fed into a machine which has rollers with teeth on them.

The teeth pull the fibres through narrow slots.

Cotton fibres are sent to cotton mills where they will be spun and woven into cloth.

SPINNING DEPT.

The USA is one of the main producers of cotton. Can you find it on a map?

Did you know...?
Malaysia is the world's largest producer of rubber.

Making rubber

Rubber is not a fabric, but it is a useful plant material. It is made from a milky liquid found in trees which first grew wild in the Amazon rain forests in South America.

South American Indians have been making rubber for hundreds of years. In the 1860s, seeds were brought from South America and planted in parts of Asia, which have a similar climate.

The liquid 'latex' is removed from the tree by cutting a slit in the bark (tapping). The latex runs out into a collecting cup fixed to the tree. All the latex is collected and taken to a factory. It is made into sheets of rubber.

Rubber is a waterproof material. It is stretchy and strong. It is made into wellington boots, the soles of shoes and elastic, for example. How many other rubber products can you think of?

35

More about: cotton fabric pp38-41 spinning and weaving pp33, 36-37, 39

Materials from animals

Wool is an animal fibre. Most of our wool comes from sheep, but the cashmere goat and the llama also have woolly coats.

Wool is warm and soft to wear. The fibres are quite long so it is easy to spin. Wool is also waterproof. Each fibre is covered with tiny overlapping scales. Water rolls off the wool along these scales.

Wool is sold to woollen mills where it will be cleaned and spun. Some is woven into cloth. Some is knitted into sweaters and other garments.

Making silk

Most fibres have to be twisted together to make a long thread. Silk is different.

Silk is produced by a caterpillar called the silkworm.

During the change from silkworm to moth, the caterpillar spins a special **cocoon** around itself from one long silk thread.

There are two types of silk moth, the domesticated silk moth shown in the picture, and the wild Tussah moth.

The largest sheep farms are in Australia and New Zealand. The sheep's **fleece** (woollen coat) is cut off in one piece. This is called shearing. Sheep are shorn once a year. The sheep's coat grows back in time for winter.

Did you know...?

A good shearer takes only 5 minutes to shear each sheep and can shear 125 sheep in a day.

On the silk farm

When the long thread is unravelled, five threads are spun together to make one strong enough for weaving into silk cloth.

Silkworms kept on silk farms, mainly in Japan, China and India, eat leaves from the mulberry tree before spinning their cocoons. Developing moths are killed with hot air or steam to stop them breaking the silk thread.

The leather and fur trade

Leather is made from the skins of cattle, sheep and pigs, also from crocodiles, lizards and snakes. All the fur or hair is removed.

The skin is then covered with a special liquid called tannin. This stops the skin decaying and makes it smooth and flexible. Some leather is polished or oiled to bring up the shine.

The animals which give us leather and furs have to be killed because the whole skin is used.

What is being made from leather in this picture?

Many animals such as leopards and cheetahs have been killed for their furs. These animals are in danger of dying out because so many have been killed for their skins.

37

More about: fabrics pp32, 34, 38-41 spinning and weaving pp33, 34, 39

Fabrics made by people

Fabrics made from natural fibres are comfortable to wear but they are not easy to care for.

> Cotton creases easily.

> Wool shrinks if it is not washed carefully.

Manufactured or synthetic fabrics can be made to order. Sometimes, they are not as comfortable as the real thing.

> Some synthetic fibres do not need ironing at all.

> They can be washed without shrinking or losing their shape.

Cotton growers and sheep farmers cannot always supply as much cotton and wool as people need. That makes the fabrics expensive.

Clothes are often made from a mixture of natural and synthetic fibres. They are comfortable and also easy to care for.

There are two main groups of manufactured fibres. Synthetic fibres are made from coal and oil. Other manufactured fibres are made by using a special process on plant fibres.

Fibres from coal and oil

Nylon, polyester and acrylic are made from substances found in coal and oil. The substances are heated until they form a liquid.

The liquid is forced through a machine with tiny holes in it, called a spinneret. The long threads are cooled until they harden.

The threads are spun and woven in the same way as natural fibres.

Fibres from plants

Viscose is made from **cellulose**. Cellulose comes from the woody part of plants. It is mixed with water, and substances are added to dissolve the cellulose.

It is made into sheets and mixed with more substances. It forms a thick liquid which can be forced through a spinneret. Acetate is also made from cellulose.

Mixing the fibres

Polyester is a light fabric. Acrylic is heavier. Nylon is a slippery material.

If you look at the labels on your clothes, you can see how natural and manufactured fibres are often mixed together.

Wool mixed with acrylic can be washed in a washing machine without shrinking or matting. Acrylic also makes the garment more hard-wearing.

Cotton is mixed with polyester to make shirts, blouses and dresses. It feels almost like cotton but it does not crease as easily and is easy to iron. Cotton can also be mixed with acrylic to make a heavier fabric.

39

More about: cotton pp32, 34-35, 40-41 oil pp20-21 wool pp32-33, 36

Which fabric?

You can probably find a lot of articles made from cotton and wool, or synthetic mixtures. You may not be able to recognise all of them, though.

Cotton fabrics

Towels are made from cotton fibres. They are **absorbent** so they soak up water.

Velvet is a type of cotton. It looks more elegant than plain cotton.

Denim is a hard-wearing cotton. It was first used to make working clothes such as jeans and overalls. Today, people wear jeans to be comfortable and fashionable, too.

Woollen fabrics

Wool can be made into a smooth fabric called worsted which is used to make business suits.

Wool is also woven into heavy fabrics such as tweed.

Special finishes

Most fabrics are given a special 'finish'. This may make them easier to iron or difficult to crease. It may make them drip-dry, so they do not need ironing. Wool can be treated to protect it from moths. Fabrics can be pre-shrunk so that they do not shrink when they are washed. The cloth is pulled to stretch the fibres, then washed. The fibres shrink back and will not shrink any more when the cloth is washed.

Corduroy, gabardine and canvas are other cotton fabrics which have been treated in a special way.

corduroy

gabardine

canvas

Did you know...?

Denim is named after the town of Nimes in France, where it was first made. The fabric was called 'serge de Nimes'.

Synthetic rubber

We need rubber for many things like car tyres, clothes and shoes. Artificial rubber is made using substances from oil. They are made into a liquid and moulded in the same way as real rubber.

Waterproofing

Fabrics can be made waterproof by coating them with plastic in a bath of plastic paste. Then they are heated to make the plastic spread through the cloth and cooled to harden the plastic.

Waterproofed cotton is made into tents and raincoats. Cloth can also be waterproofed with rubber and wax.

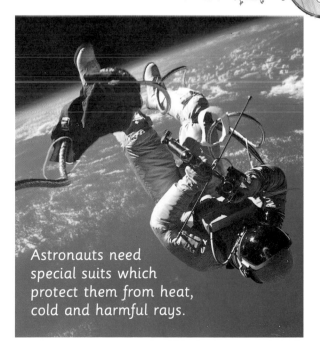

Astronauts need special suits which protect them from heat, cold and harmful rays.

Firefighters and racing drivers need clothes which do not burn. Fabrics for their clothes are treated to make them fireproof.

41

More about: cotton pp34-35, 38-39   rubber p35   wool pp36, 38-39

One room, many materials

Each room in the house is full of interesting materials, particularly the bathroom.

Modern baths are often made from plastic. A thick plastic sheet is laid over a bath-shaped mould and heated. The sheet is sucked down into the mould.

The shower curtain is made of plastic or a waterproofed fabric.

Plastic-coated wallpapers do not absorb water vapour. They can be wiped dry.

If the walls are tiled, water can be wiped off them.

There might be special materials, such as a sponge, a loofah or a pumice stone.

Hot and cold water flows from taps.

Glass jars contain creams.

Talcum powder, hair spray and shaving foam are in tins.

Plastic bottles hold shampoo and other liquids.

Find out about mirrors in the *New Horizons* book, *Energy, forces and communication.*

A toothbrush has a plastic handle. The brush may be made of nylon or **bristles**.

A medicine cupboard contains medicines, cotton wool and sticking plaster.

Toothpaste is held in a plastic tube.

Towels, flannels and bath mats are made from absorbent fabrics.

Which of these things are solid and which are liquid? Are any of them gases?

Medicine cupboards should be high on the wall or locked. This is to stop young children taking things which might be harmful.

43

More about: oil products pp20-21, 39, 47 soap p46 sponge p44

Sponge, loofah and pumice

Sponge

A real sponge is an animal which lives its life in the sea stuck to a rock. It has a soft body without a backbone.

The sponge's **skeleton** is a mass of fibres with small holes in between. When the animal dies, its skeleton is left behind. Sponges are sometimes found in groups. A bath sponge is a skeleton from a group of sponges.

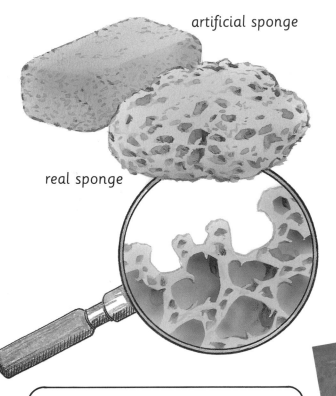

artificial sponge

real sponge

Sponges are very absorbent. They soak up water until they are full.

Divers gather sponges from the rocks. Most come from the seas around the Greek islands.

Loofah

A loofah is made from a vegetable. Another name for it is the vegetable sponge. It is the skeleton of a tropical plant called the dishcloth gourd.

The **pulp** and seeds of the fruit are removed to make a loofah. This leaves a spongy skeleton made of fibres.

Pumice

Pumice is a grey rock which comes from **volcanoes**. People use it to remove stains and dry skin from their bodies.

Pumice is very light and full of tiny holes.

When a volcano **erupts**, melted rock called **lava** pours out. When the lava meets the cold air, it hardens into rock. This is pumice.

Floating and sinking

Collect different objects and test them to see which float and which sink. Do they all float? Are they solid or hollow? What happens if you fill them with water?

Why does a large ship float, but a small stone sink?

What makes an object float or sink? Find out in the *New Horizons* book, *Energy, forces and communication*.

45

More about: baths p42 fibres pp32-41 water pp25, 28-29, 50-51

Soaps, creams and powders

You can wash with water on its own, but it is much easier with soap.

Try this test. Run the tap until the water is warm and hold your hand under it. Turn off the tap and look at your hand. The water lies on it in drops with dry bits in between. The drops soon disappear. Now, rub some soap on to your hand and hold it under the tap again. This time, the water spreads all over your hand. Your hand stays wet.

Water seems to have a sort of 'skin' that makes it hold itself together in drops.

Soap breaks down the 'skin' and makes the water spread. When the surface 'skin' has been broken, dirt can pass through into the water more easily.

Soap is made from a mixture of fat, minerals such as soda, and **lanolin** from sheep's wool. Lanolin is a natural grease that is washed out at the woollen mill. It is also used to make creams and lotions.

This pondskater can walk on the surface 'skin' of the water.

Talcum powder is a natural substance. Talc is the softest mineral. Rocks containing it are mined and sent to factories. There the talc is ground into a powder and scent may be added.

Using plants

Some shampoos, **cosmetics** and medicines are made from plant materials.

Shampoo may contain **henna** which grows in Egypt and India. It dyes hair red.

Some shampoos contain plant oils such as almond to soften hair.

Cough sweets are made from plants such as **eucalyptus**, a gum tree which first grew in Australia . . .

. . . or **menthol** which comes from the peppermint plant.

Witch hazel is a small tree which first grew in Asia and North America. Witch hazel lotion reduces swelling.

What is make-up?

People have been using make-up or cosmetics for thousands of years.

Ancient Egyptians drew round their eyes with **kohl**. This is a powder made from a mineral in rock. They dyed their hair with henna.

Ancient Greeks and Romans used face powder and **rouge** for reddening their cheeks. Some cosmetics were made from lead which is poisonous.

Ancient Britons sometimes painted themselves with woad. This was a blue dye from the leaves of the woad plant.

North American Indians painted their faces with warpaint before a battle.

Modern face powder is a mixture of talc and other minerals. Lipstick is made from oils which do not dry out. Creams and lotions are made from waxes and oils which stop the skin drying out.

What other plants can you find in the soaps, creams, powders and lotions in your bathroom?

47

More about: minerals pp4-5 water pp25, 28-29, 50-51

In the bathroom

If you run a hot bath or shower and the water is really hot, billows of water vapour fill the bathroom. You have to add cold water so that you can get into your bath or shower.

A cold bathroom with bad **ventilation** is the worst for condensation. Vapour condenses more quickly in cold air.

Condensation can be a problem in a bathroom because it makes everything feel damp.

Condensation runs down walls and windows. The water soaks into ordinary wallpaper. Damp patches form and the paper peels off the wall. Water also soaks into wooden window frames which are not properly protected by paint and rots the wood.

When vapour hits the cold surfaces of walls, windows and mirrors, it turns back into water. This is called **condensation**.

Ventilation gets rid of the water vapour before it has a chance to condense.

An **extractor fan** sucks water vapour out of the room.

Vinyl is a type of plastic which can be added to paint or used to coat wallpaper. Water cannot soak through vinyl. It runs down the surface and can be wiped off.

Air from an open window blows water vapour away.

Water and you

What happens to the temperature of your body when you have a bath? When you get undressed, you may feel a bit cold. You feel warmer in the hot water.

Tiles are made from fired clay which is decorated and **glazed**. Glaze is made from silica and other minerals. The glaze dries hard and makes the tiles waterproof.

When you get out, your body is wet. The water begins to evaporate and this makes your body feel cold again.

49

More about: clay pp6, 8, 12-13 silica p13 window frames pp11, 16

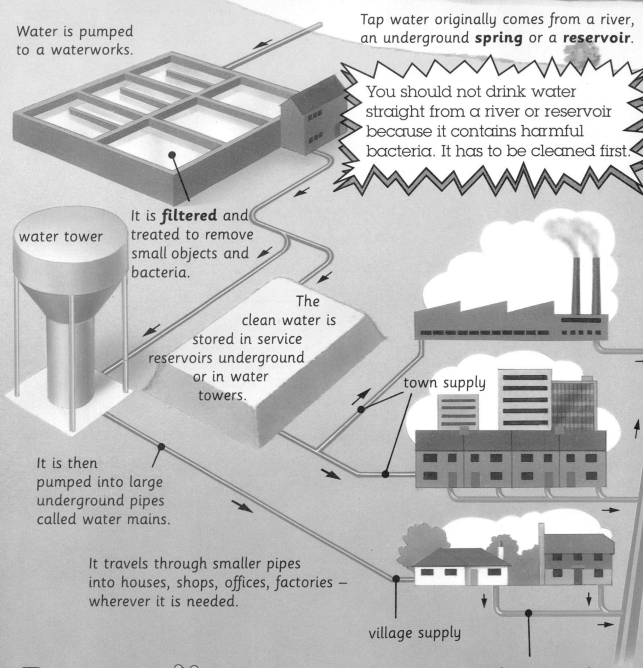

Water is pumped to a waterworks.

Tap water originally comes from a river, an underground **spring** or a **reservoir**.

You should not drink water straight from a river or reservoir because it contains harmful bacteria. It has to be cleaned first.

water tower

It is **filtered** and treated to remove small objects and bacteria.

The clean water is stored in service reservoirs underground or in water towers.

town supply

It is then pumped into large underground pipes called water mains.

It travels through smaller pipes into houses, shops, offices, factories — wherever it is needed.

village supply

When you wash up or have a bath, the dirty water goes down the drain. Waste from sinks, baths and lavatories is called **sewage**.

Recycling water

When you turn on a tap, clean water comes out.

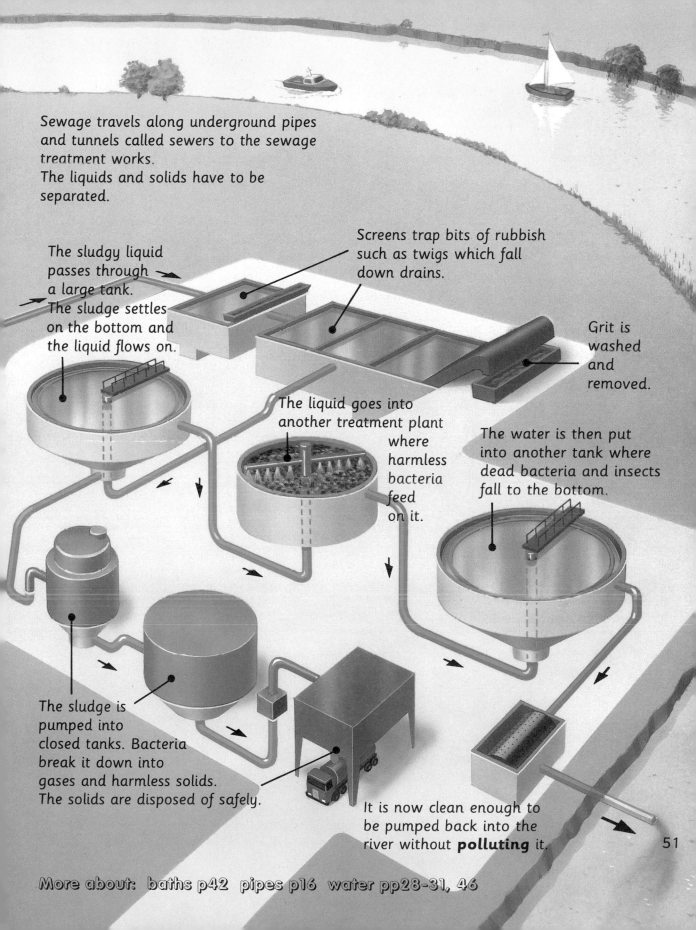

Sewage travels along underground pipes
and tunnels called sewers to the sewage
treatment works.
The liquids and solids have to be
separated.

Screens trap bits of rubbish
such as twigs which fall
down drains.

The sludgy liquid
passes through
a large tank.
The sludge settles
on the bottom and
the liquid flows on.

Grit is
washed
and
removed.

The liquid goes into
another treatment plant
where
harmless
bacteria
feed
on it.

The water is then put
into another tank where
dead bacteria and insects
fall to the bottom.

The sludge is
pumped into
closed tanks. Bacteria
break it down into
gases and harmless solids.
The solids are disposed of safely.

It is now clean enough to
be pumped back into the
river without **polluting** it.

51

More about: baths p42 pipes p16 water pp28-31, 46

Packaging materials

Many of the things we buy are **packaged**. Different materials are used to suit different objects.

Food is packaged in many different ways. You can buy tins, bottles, jars, boxes. What other types of food packaging can you find?

Fresh foods can go bad if they are left uncovered in the air. Some foods are 'shrink-wrapped' to keep the air out.

Yogurt, cream and some soft cheeses are sold in moulded plastic containers.

Shrink-wrapping

A sheet of plastic film is heated and stretched. When it cools, it is wrapped round the food so that no air can get in.

The wrapped food passes through a heated tunnel. The plastic softens and shrinks back to its original size. It is wrapped round the food tightly.

Moulding pots

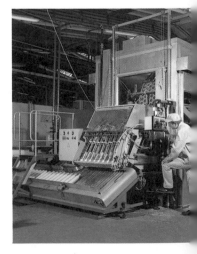

A plastic sheet on top of a mould is heated until it is soft. Air is sucked out through holes in the mould. The soft plastic is pulled down into the shape of the mould and cooled to harden it.

Milk is sold in glass bottles or in paper cartons. The paper is coated with wax to stop the milk seeping through. You can also buy fruit juices and other liquids in wax-covered cartons.

How much does it hold?

Liquids are sold by volume. Manufacturers show this in litres (l) and millilitres (ml). Solids are sold by **mass**. This is shown in grams (g) and kilograms (kg).

If you go to buy loose tomatoes, you can weigh out the exact amount you want.

With packaged goods, shoppers want to know how much the package contains. Packaged goods have to state the amount on the outside.

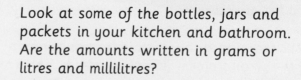

Look at some of the bottles, jars and packets in your kitchen and bathroom. Are the amounts written in grams or litres and millilitres?

53

More about: glass pp6, 13, 61 moulding plastic pp20-21, 42

Throwing things away

When materials are too old to be used any more, they are thrown away. Their packaging is thrown away, too. Some of this becomes rubbish, some becomes **litter**.

Suppose you buy fish and chips and a can of drink. If you throw the papers and empty can into the dustbin, they are rubbish. They have been thrown away in the proper place. If you throw them down on the street, they become litter.

Litter is rubbish which is thrown away in the wrong place. It makes streets, parks and other public places look untidy.

54

How can you stop people spoiling the countryside with their litter? Draw a poster showing your ideas.

LITTER BUGS! ME!

Two sorts of rubbish

If you throw away some orange peel, it will gradually **decay**. This is called **biodegradable** waste. Plants and animals are biodegradable.

THE DAILY HORIZON

Slipping and sinking | Freezing conditions cause havoc on the roads

Did you know...?

Paper is biodegradable, but some newspapers can still be read 60 years after being buried in a rubbish tip.

As soon as it falls from the tree or someone picks it, the apple dies.

If you eat it straight away, it tastes good and fresh.

An apple growing on a tree is alive.

If you leave it lying around, it begins to decay. The skin becomes wrinkled and brown patches appear. . .

. . . until it becomes brown all over and begins to fall apart. This happens because bacteria break it down.

If you throw down a plastic bag or carton, it will not rot away. It will stay there for ever unless someone picks it up. This non-biodegradable waste can harm animals. Always put waste in a bin or take it home.

Find out more about how dead plants and animals decay in the *New Horizons* book, *Life around us*.

55

More about: packaging pp52-53, 57, 60-61 waste disposal pp56-57

Refuse disposal

The rubbish you throw away in the dustbin is called refuse. What happens to it?

Collecting household refuse

Refuse collectors call at each house about once a week . . .

. . . and empty the dustbins into the back of a special lorry.

Machinery compresses the refuse to make it smaller so that more can be put in.

When the lorry is full, it is driven to a tip or to a land fill site where it is buried.

Most refuse is tipped. The tip may be on waste ground, or in an old quarry or gravel pit.

When a tip is full, it is covered with soil so that the land can be used again.

56

Getting rid of other refuse

Offices, shops, schools, hospitals, hotels and blocks of flats have a lot of refuse. Ordinary dustbins would soon fill up. Extra-large bins are lifted and emptied by automatic machinery on the refuse lorry.

Most towns have a 'civic amenity site' where people can take rubbish that is too big for the dustbin.

Litter bins in towns and villages are emptied by street cleaners who tip the rubbish into handcarts. Street cleaners also sweep up litter from the streets. They empty their carts into refuse lorries which meet them two or three times a day.

Waste from factories

Think how much rubbish there is from factories! There is rubbish thrown away by people who work there. There is material left over from making products. There is left-over and waste wrapping and packaging.

This 'industrial waste' is usually collected by private rubbish disposal firms. Some factory wastes can be cleaned and recycled, though.

Did you know...?
Of all the things we throw away, 80% could be recycled.

Street cleaning machines suck up rubbish from road edges and gutters.

More about: packaging pp52-53, 55 recycling pp50-51, 58-61

Recycling wastes

If you look in your dustbin at home, you can see that a lot of the rubbish is packaging made from paper and cardboard. Paper and card need not be wasted. They can be re-used or recycled. So can some metals, glass, wood, fabrics, some plastics and used motor oil.

Making paper

1 Paper is made from trees. When they have been chopped down, they are taken to a pulp mill.

2 The wood is ground into tiny pieces and mixed with water to make pulp. The pulp goes to a paper mill where it is mixed with water and other substances. Hemp or jute fibres are sometimes added to make the paper stronger or thicker.

Did you know...?

Paper was invented by the Chinese over 2000 years ago. Until about 100 years ago, pulp was made from old rags which were boiled and left to rot, then shredded.

3 This mixture, called the 'stuff', is put on to the paper-making machine. First, it is spread into a thin layer on a moving belt made of wire or plastic mesh. Some of the water is drawn out.

On average, every person throws away two trees' worth of paper each year. New York in the USA has to get rid of 24 000 tonnes of rubbish every day!

Recycling paper

Recycled paper is made from waste paper instead of wood. So, fewer trees have to be chopped down. It is far quicker and cheaper to make pulp from paper than it is to chop down trees and grind up the wood.

5 At the end of the machine, it is given a final drying with steam-heat. It then passes through heavy rollers which give it a smooth finish.

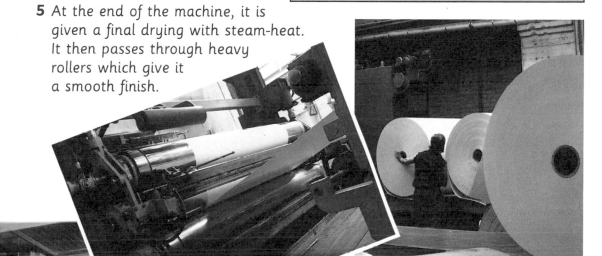

6 Finally, the paper is wound into huge rolls, ready to leave the mill.

How many uses can you find for paper? Would recycled paper be as good for all these things?

4 Most of the remaining water is squeezed out by a series of rollers as the pulp moves along the machine.

59

More about: recycling pp50-51, 60-61 wood pp18-19

Recycling metal

Nearly all food and pet food cans are made from steel. Four-fifths of all drinks cans worldwide are made from aluminium.

Aluminium is produced from bauxite, a soft, crumbly ore. It is found all over the world, but Australia has the most. Making new aluminium from bauxite is expensive, so producers are encouraged to recycle as much as they can.

Do you know where to find steel can collection skips? There are also places where you can leave aluminium cans, old newspapers, and plastic for recycling.

Did you know...?

- It takes 20 times more energy to make new aluminium than to recycle it. It takes 4 times more energy to make new steel than to recycle it.
- Aluminium cans are the most recycled in the world – over 50 billion in 1990!

Sorting metals

Metals have to be sorted before they can be recycled. Steel is **magnetic** – it is attracted to a magnet. Aluminium cans are not magnetic. At waste treatment sites, huge magnets are used to sort steel cans from aluminium cans.

Recycling glass

Have you seen bottle banks where you can throw away empty bottles? The glass is melted down at a glass factory and made into new products.

Biodegradable waste can be recycled by putting it on a compost heap. Find out about them in the *New Horizons* book, *Life around us*.

Cans are taken to factories where they are melted down and used to make more cans. The same metal can be used again and again.

Recycling is important

Throwing rubbish away is expensive and causes pollution. It costs millions of pounds a year to collect and get rid of rubbish. Recycling saves money and helps protect the environment. It also means Earth's raw materials and energy sources will last longer.

Find out more about magnets in the *New Horizons* book, *Energy, forces and communication*.

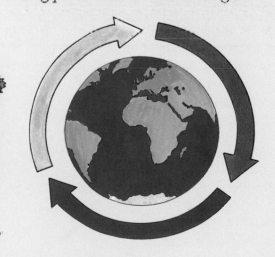

61

More about: plastic pp20-21, 42, 52   rubbish disposal pp56-57

Key words

The meanings of words can depend on how and when they are used. You may find that as you learn more about science the meanings change slightly.

absorbent can soak up liquid

acid a sharp, sour-tasting substance; vinegar and lemon juice contain acids

aggregate any material mixed with cement to form concrete

arteries tubes in the body which carry blood away from the heart

bacteria very tiny living things which are all around us. Some cause disease

biodegradable materials which rot away

blast furnace a huge 'oven' used in steel-making

bond to join together

bristles short, stiff hairs

carbon dioxide one of the gases in air

cast to shape in a mould

cellulose fibres made from the woody part of plants

churn a vessel for holding milk or for making cream into butter

climate the usual weather conditions of an area or country

cocoon the silk case a caterpillar spins around itself when it is ready to turn into a butterfly or a moth

compress to squeeze tightly together

condensation water drops which form when water vapour cools

cosmetics substances for making the skin or hair look different

crystals small glass-like pieces which are all the same shape

decay to rot

defrost to thaw out from frozen

diet the different foods you eat

dissolve to seem to disappear when stirred into a liquid; to break down into very small parts in a liquid

domesticate to tame a wild animal

erupt to burst out

eucalyptus gum tree, from Australia

evaporate to turn into vapour

excavator a machine for digging out large amounts of earth and other materials

expand to get bigger or swell

export to sell goods to another country

extractor fan a fan which draws out or extracts air from a room

extrusion a method of shaping by forcing a substance through a machine

fabric cloth

fermentation a process in which one substance works on another to change it, such as yeast changing sugar into alcohol

fibres thin threads

filter to remove solid bits from liquid by pouring it through a mesh, cloth or paper

finish the final treatment on cloth or other materials after manufacture

fleece the whole woollen coat of a sheep

flexible bendy

foundations concrete base which supports a wall to stop it sinking into the ground

fuel a substance which burns to release energy to make things work

fungus a plant which can grow without light such as a mushroom or mould

fuse to melt and join together by heat

geologist scientist who studies rocks

glaze to coat with a glassy substance making the surface shiny and waterproof

gravel small stones

hardwood strong wood from trees such as oak and beech

henna a plant which first came from Egypt. Its leaves are made into a red dye

import to buy goods from another country

insulation a layer of foam or other material which prevents heat escaping

kiln an oven for baking clay

kohl a powder used for darkening eyelids

lanolin grease from sheep's wool, which is used for cosmetics

lava hot, melted rock which pours out of a volcano when it erupts

litter rubbish which has been thrown away in the wrong place

magnetic metal such as iron and steel which is attracted to a magnet

maize Indian corn

manufactured made by people

mass the amount of matter in an object, measured in grams (g) and kilograms (kg)

menthol substance from peppermint plants

mineral any natural substance found in the ground which has not been formed from plants or animals. Rocks and metals are minerals

molten melted, made liquid by heat

ore rock and earth which contains other substances such as metal

package put in boxes, bottles or paper

pasta food such as spaghetti made from a flour and water paste

pollute spoil or make dirty by people

porous full of tiny holes, like a sponge. Water can seep into porous rock or stone

preserve to prevent from going bad by special preparation such as pickling

processed the series of changes which takes place when something is made or treated in a factory

pulp a soft wet mass, such as the wood and water mixture used in paper-making

pure not mixed with other substances

quarry a place from where minerals or stone are cut

refinery a place where oil from the ground is made into products such as petrol

reinforce to strengthen

reservoir a large lake where water is collected and stored

rouge cosmetic which reddens the cheeks

rust reddish-brown coating which forms on some metals when they are left wet. Rust gradually eats away the metal

sawmill a place where wood is sawn into planks, ready for sale

season to dry out wood in a kiln or by letting air circulate around it

sewage waste matter and water carried away from buildings in sewer pipes

sewers underground pipes or tunnels carrying sewage

silica tiny glass-like grains in sand

skeleton a framework of bones or fibres which supports the body of an animal or, sometimes, a plant

softwood light, soft wood from trees such as pines and firs

spring a place where water flows out of rock; often the start of a river

spin to draw out fibres and twist them into a long thread

survey to measure or examine closely

synthetic artificial; made by people

temperate climate of four seasons, with warm summers and cold winters

temperature the measurement of how hot something is

transparent see-through, like glass

treated to apply a process or a substance to a material to change it in some way

tropical from the hottest part of the Earth's surface near the equator

ventilation the flow of air into a room

vitamins substances, found in foods, which are essential for good health

volcano place where melted rock bursts through the surface of Earth. The build-up of cooled rock forms a mountain

warp to bend or twist

yeast a type of fungus which makes bread dough rise and turns sugar into alcohol

Index